STAR WARS

ADVENTURES

LUKE SKYWALKER AND THE
TREASURE OF THE DRAGONSNAKES

Designer
David Nestelle

Assistant Editor
Freddye Lins

Editor
Randy Stradley

Publisher
Mike Richardson

Special thanks to Elaine Mederer, Jann Moorhead, David Anderman,
Leland Chee, Sue Rostoni, and Carol Roeder at Lucas Licensing

STAR WARS ADVENTURES: LUKE SKYWALKER AND THE TREASURE OF THE DRAGONSNAKES

ISBN: 9781848564008

Published by Titan Books, a division of Titan Publishing Group Ltd.
144 Southwark Street, London SE1 0UP

Originally published by Dark Horse Comics.

First edition: February 2010

10 9 8 7 6 5 4 3 2 1

Printed in Lithuania

LUKE SKYWALKER AND THE TREASURE OF THE DRAGONSNAKES

Script **Tom Taylor**

Art **Daxiong**

Lettering **Michael Heisler**

Cover art **Daxiong**

TITAN BOOKS

**THIS STORY TAKES PLACE DURING
STAR WARS: THE EMPIRE STRIKES BACK.**

IN A DEEP SWAMP ON DAGOBAH, THEY LIE IN THE DARKNESS.

WAITING FOR AN OPPORTUNITY TO FEED.

THE KING OF THE DRAGONSNAKES IS THE LARGEST OF HIS KIND. HIS STRENGTH IS IMMENSE.

THE KING STRIKES WITH FURY AND PRECISION.

NOTHING ESCAPES HIS JAWS.

THE OTHER DRAGONSNAKES LIVE ONLY OFF OF THE SCRAPS THE KING LEAVES BEHIND.

THIS IS HOW IT IS.

THIS IS HOW IT HAS BEEN.

UNTIL...

RRRRRROOOOOOOOO

NO, ARTOO, YOU STAY PUT. I'LL HAVE A LOOK AROUND --

ARTOO?

WOOWEEEEEEEEE.

THE KING IS HIT BY SOMETHING THAT DROPS FROM THE SKY INTO HIS SWAMP. SOMETHING THAT SHOULD NOT BE.

THE OTHER DRAGONSNAKES SCATTER. BUT THE KING DOES NOT HIDE...

THE KING SENSES MOTION IN THE WATER...

YOU BE MORE CAREFUL, ARTOO -- THAT WAY!

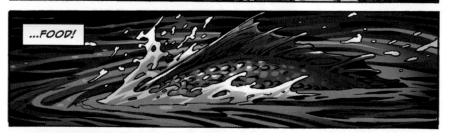

...FOOD!

THE KING'S TEETH CLOSE ON HIS HELPLESS PREY. BUT IT TASTES...WRONG. IT IS TOO HARD EVEN FOR KING'S MIGHTY JAWS. A TOOTH BREAKS. THE THING **WON'T STOP BEEPING.**

YOU'RE LUCKY YOU DON'T TASTE VERY GOOD. ANYTHING BROKEN?

HMMM.

HE WATCHES THE OTHER ONE. SOFTER, NO DOUBT TASTIER.

DRAGONSNAKES ARE PATIENT—

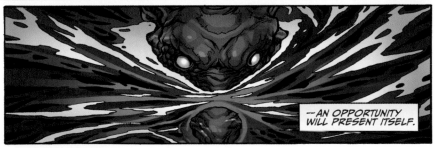

—AN OPPORTUNITY WILL PRESENT ITSELF.

BUT OVER THE NEXT FEW DAYS, AN OPPORTUNITY DOES NOT PRESENT ITSELF. INSTEAD, THE SOFTER ONE STAYS ON THE LAND.

RUN! YES. A JEDI'S STRENGTH FLOWS FROM THE FORCE. BUT BEWARE OF THE DARK SIDE.

ANGER...FEAR ...AGGRESSION. THE DARK SIDE OF THE FORCE ARE THEY.

EASILY THEY FLOW, QUICK TO JOIN YOU IN A FIGHT...

BUT DRAGONSNAKES ARE PATIENT.

UNH!

FALL, YOU DID.

THANKS FOR THAT.

STUBBORN AND HARD IS YOUR HEAD. SOFTEN IT WE WILL.

I STOOD ON MY HEAD TO SOFTEN IT?

MYSTERIOUS ARE THE WAYS OF THE FORCE.

DID YOU JUST MAKE ME STAND ON MY HEAD FOR *TWO HOURS* BECAUSE I WAS *ANNOYING* YOU?

VERY MYSTERIOUS.

19

"BEYOND THE SWAMPS.

"BEYOND THE FORESTS.

"A PLACE THERE IS WHERE NO TREE GROWS.

"A CRAGGY, JAGGED PLACE IT IS. DANGEROUS.

"DANGEROUS ALSO ARE THE CREATURES THAT LIVE THERE. CREATURES THAT COULD NOT LIVE AMONGST THEIR OWN KIND. BANISHED THEY ARE TO THE JAGGED PLACE.

22

FOLLOW THE DRAGONSNAKE FROM HERE WE SHOULD.

HOW DO WE FOLLOW HIM? WE DON'T EVEN KNOW WHERE HE IS.

THIS IS WHERE HE FEEDS.

OPPORTUNITY. THE KING'S PATIENCE IS REWARDED.

SO WHAT? WE JUST WAIT AND HOPE THAT HE --

THOK!

HIS PREY ESCAPES INTO THE DARKNESS. THE KING DOESN'T MIND. THIS IS HIS ELEMENT. HE RULES THIS WATER.

HIS PREY WILL TASTE ALL THE SWEETER FOR THE STRUGGLE.

AND THE KING LIKES TO PLAY WITH HIS FOOD.

THE PREY NO LONGER KNOWS WHICH WAY IS UP ...OR DOWN.

IT WILL NEED AIR. IT WILL SOON BE...

...HELPLESS?

SOMETHING UNEXPECTED HAPPENS.

THERE IS LIGHT IN
THE DARKNESS...

...BUT LIGHT CANNOT HARM HIM.
ONE CRUSHING BITE FROM HIS
JAWS AND THE KING'S PREY
WILL BE FINISHED.

JUST ONE BITE...

VSSSSSHH!

PAIN! PAIN SUCH AS THE KING HAS NEVER FELT.

REEEEAAARR!

IN HIS FURY, THE KING STRIKES AT THE FIRST THING HE SEES.

BOOOWOOO!

SNAP!

WOOT.

BWOOP.

IT WAS. YES.

MUCH FUN.

HUMBLED WAS THE KING OF THE DRAGONSNAKES --

"-- AND WITNESSED IT, DID THE OTHER DRAGONSNAKES.

"FAILED FOR THE FIRST TIME IN THEIR MEMORY --

"-- SHOWN WEAKNESS, HAS THE KING.

"LIKE THEIR REACTION, HE DOES NOT."

FOUND HIM YOU DID. WELL DONE.

AN ADVENTURE YOU HAVE ALREADY HAD -- YET YOU ARE WHERE YOU STARTED.

SOMETIMES... *HUFF...*YOUR "OBSERVATIONS" ...*HFF...*AREN'T HELPFUL.

-: *GASP!* :-

HUFF... THANKS...

I'M SLEEPING INSIDE A GIANT SPIDER?

YOU ARE NOT SLEEPING YET, BUT SOON, HOPEFULLY.

SLEEP WELL.

YOUR LIGHTSABER, USE IT.

WHAT? I CAN'T *FIGHT* YOU, MASTER!

DEFEND YOURSELF!

THUMP

ALL RIGHT! BUT I DON'T WANT TO HURT YOU.

VRMMMMM

LET *ME* WORRY ABOUT THAT, YOU SHOULD.

HNGH.

VRRRRRRNNNNNRRRNNNN

HA!

I DID IT!

HMMPH... ONLY BEAT A STICK YOU DID.

COME--

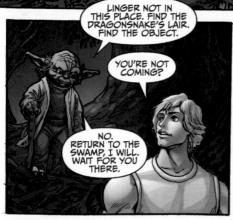

50

LUKE IS BEING WATCHED. HE CAN FEEL THE CREATURES THAT DWELL HERE. HE CAN FEEL THEIR EYES ON HIM.

THEY ARE HUNGRY AND VIOLENT.

THEY ARE WATCHING HIM. ASSESSING HIM. HIS BOLDNESS STEPPING INTO THIS PLACE HAS BOUGHT HIM A MOMENT --

-- BUT THAT MOMENT HAS PASSED.

A LIGHTSABER IS A GOOD WEAPON.

BUT THERE IS A TIME TO FIGHT--

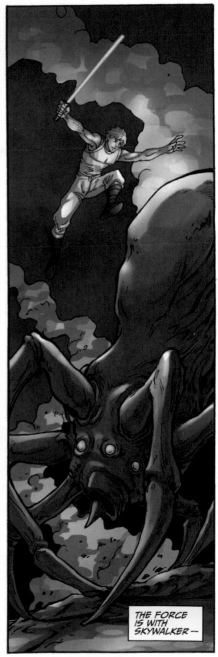

53

--BUT HE WILL NEED MORE THAN THE FORCE TO SURVIVE THIS.

THE CREATURES HOWL AND SHRIEK. THEIR CLAWS REACH, READY TO PULL LUKE LIMB FROM LIMB. THEIR FANGS ARE BARED, READY TO BITE AND TEAR.

BUT SUDDENLY...

HUH?

BEN?

EVERYTHING HURTS, BEN. THERE ARE PARTS OF ME I *NEVER KNEW I HAD* THAT HURT.

IF THE GROUND *HADN'T* GIVEN WAY FOR YOU, YOU'D BE HURTING A LOT MORE. STAND *UP*.

WHY HAVE THOSE CREATURES STOPPED ATTACKING?

EVEN THE MOST *FEARFUL* OF CREATURES MUST *FEAR* SOMETHING.

I'M BENEATH THE JAGGED PLACE. *THEY* DON'T WANT TO FOLLOW.

THE DRAGONSNAKE *IS* DOWN HERE.

RIGHT. LIKE MASTER YODA SAID...

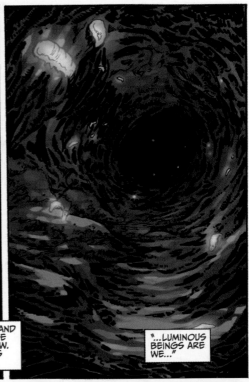

"...MY ALLY IS THE FORCE. AND A POWERFUL ALLY IT IS. LIFE CREATES IT, MAKES IT GROW. ITS ENERGY SURROUNDS US AND BINDS US...

"...LUMINOUS BEINGS ARE WE..."

THERE IS A PLACE IN THESE TUNNELS WHERE THERE IS NO LIFE.

A PLACE OF DEATH.

THE DRAGONSNAKE'S LAIR.

"A JEDI USES THE FORCE FOR KNOWLEDGE AND DEFENSE...

"...NEVER FOR ATTACK."

THE PREY HAS COME TO THE KING'S LAIR. IT HAS BROUGHT THE BURNING LIGHT.

THE KING IS ANGRY.

THE KING IS ENRAGED.

THE KING'S... FINGER HURTS.

"A FINE WEAPON A LIGHTSABER IS, BUT YOU ARE MORE THAN WHAT YOU HOLD."

"LOOK BEYOND YOUR WEAPON. LOOK TO YOURSELF."

TOOOWEEE.

DONE WELL, YOU HAVE.

THANK YOU, MASTER YODA.

I BELIEVE YOU WANTED THIS.

NOT REALLY.

HUH?

THE KING RETREATS BACK INTO HIS SWAMP.

BUT IT IS NO LONGER HIS SWAMP. THE OTHER DRAGONSNAKES HAVE SEEN HIM HUMBLED. THEY NO LONGER FEAR HIM.

DESPITE THEIR SMALLER SIZE, UNITED, THEY TURN ON HIM.

FACED WITH THIS REBELLION, THE KING FLEES.

THE KING BURROWS INTO THE DEEP MUD.

NO MATTER. THE OTHERS WILL WAIT FOR HIM.

THE DRAGONSNAKES ARE PATIENT.

THE EGG OF THE ACCIPITERO. VERY TASTY.

YOU SENT ME INTO *THAT* JUST TO GET YOUR SOUP TO TASTE...?

NO. TOO LARGE WAS THAT DRAGONSNAKE. UNBALANCED WAS THE SWAMP. THE OTHER DRAGONSNAKES SUFFERED DUE TO HIS GREED. STUNTED AND SCARED WERE THEY, SUCH WAS HIS DOMINANCE.

LIKE VADER. LIKE THE EMPEROR. LIKE THE EMPIRE.

HMM. THE SWAMP, LIKE THE GALAXY. AFRAID OF A BULLY. TOO SCARED TO RECOGNIZE *ITS* POWER.

ALSO AVAILABLE NOW:

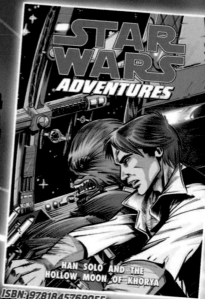

STAR WARS ADVENTURES

HAN SOLO AND THE HOLLOW MOON OF KHORYA

ISBN: 9781845769055

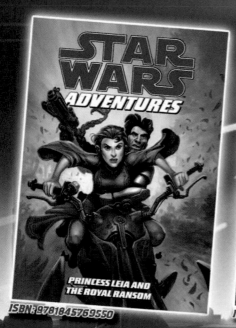

STAR WARS ADVENTURES

PRINCESS LEIA AND THE ROYAL RANSOM

ISBN: 9781845769550

STAR WARS ADVENTURES

LUKE SKYWALKER AND THE TREASURE OF THE DRAGONSNAKES

ISBN: 9781848564008

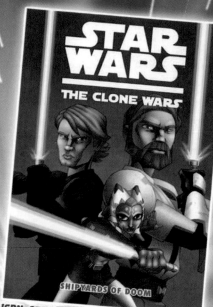

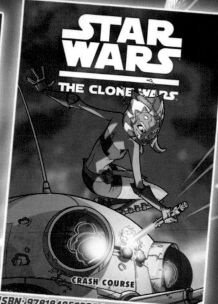

SHIPYARDS OF DOOM

ISBN: 9781848561304

CRASH COURSE

ISBN: 9781848562004

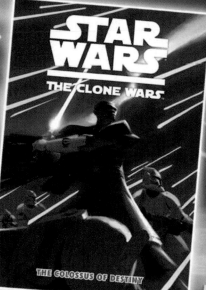

THE WIND RAIDERS OF TALORAAN

ISBN: 9781848563346

THE COLOSSUS OF DESTINY

ISBN: 9781848565371

THE FORCE IS

www.titanbooks.com

DON'T MISS THE CONTINUING BATTLE AGAINS
CLONE WARS